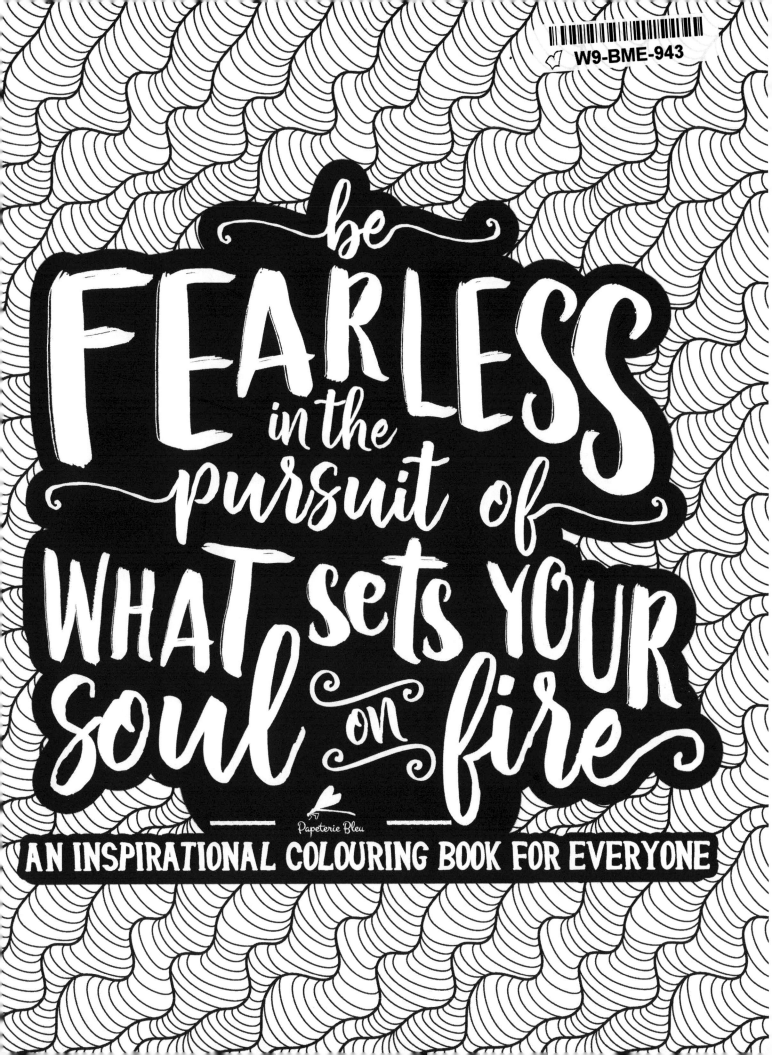

be **FEARLESS** in the pursuit of WHAT sets YOUR soul on fire

Papeterie Bleu

AN INSPIRATIONAL COLOURING BOOK FOR EVERYONE

Want free goodies?
Email us at freebies@pbleu.com

@papeteriebleu

Papeterie Bleu

Shop our other books at
www.pbleu.com

Wholesale distribution through Ingram Content Group
www.ingramcontent.com/publishers/distribution/wholesale

For questions and customer service, email us at
support@pbleu.com

FREE PDF DOWNLOAD OF THIS BOOK

www.pbleu.com/inspire

YOUR DOWNLOAD CODE: NP4569

@papeteriebleu

Papeterie Bleu

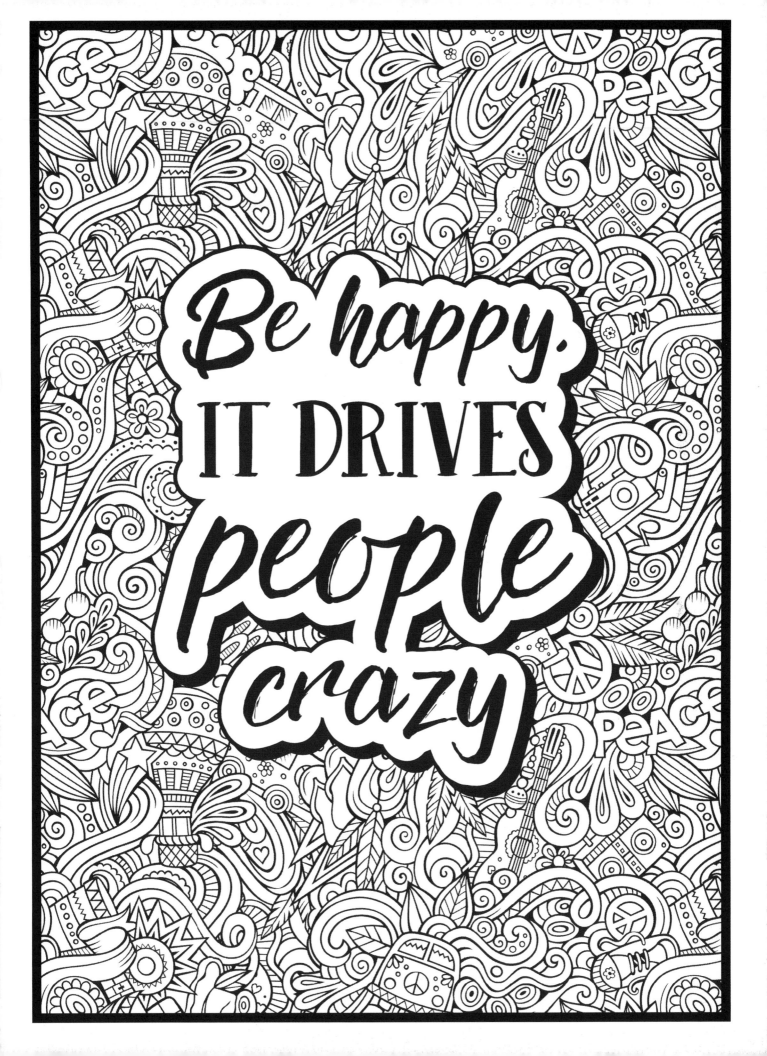

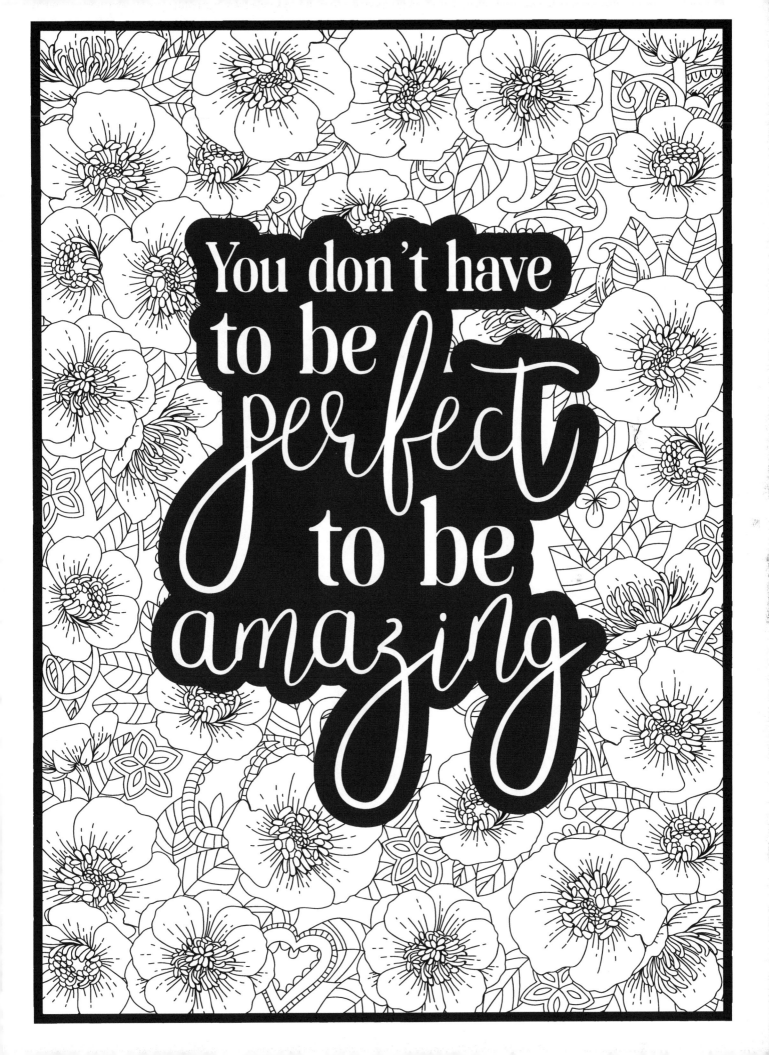

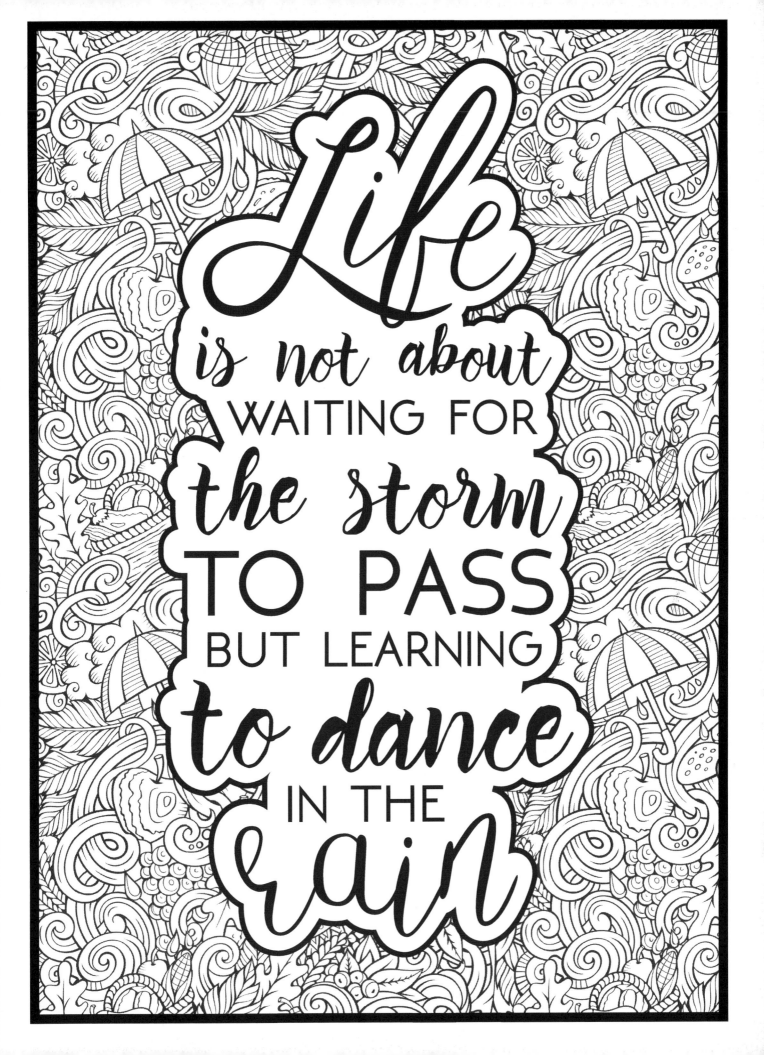

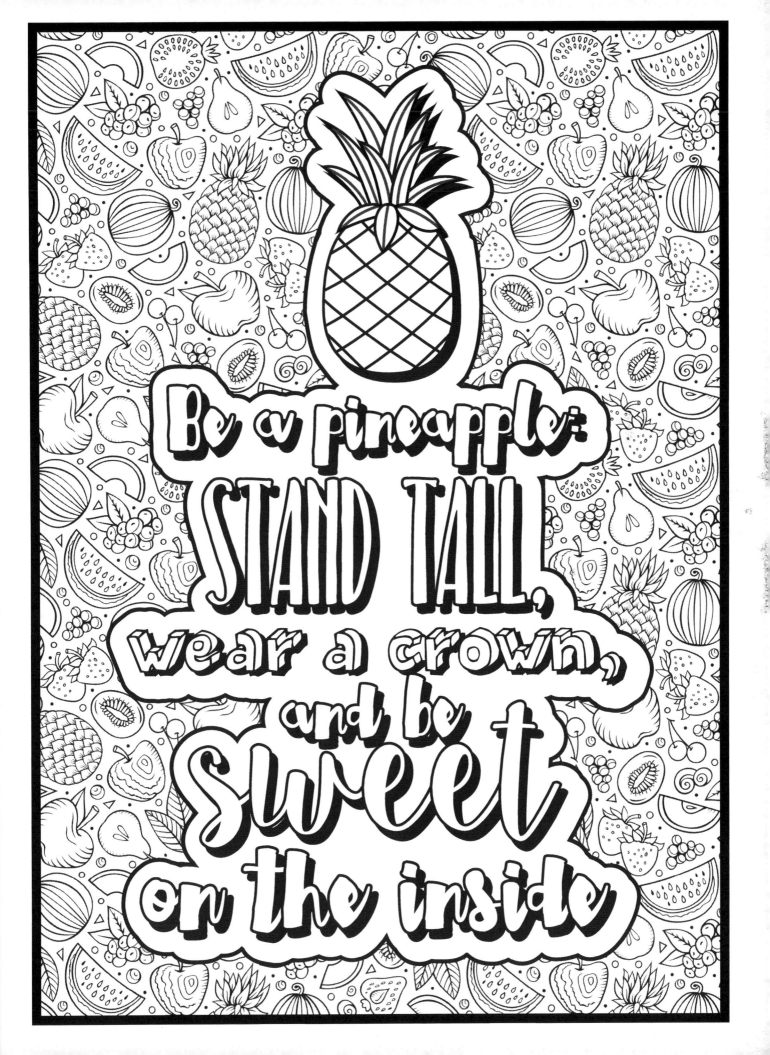

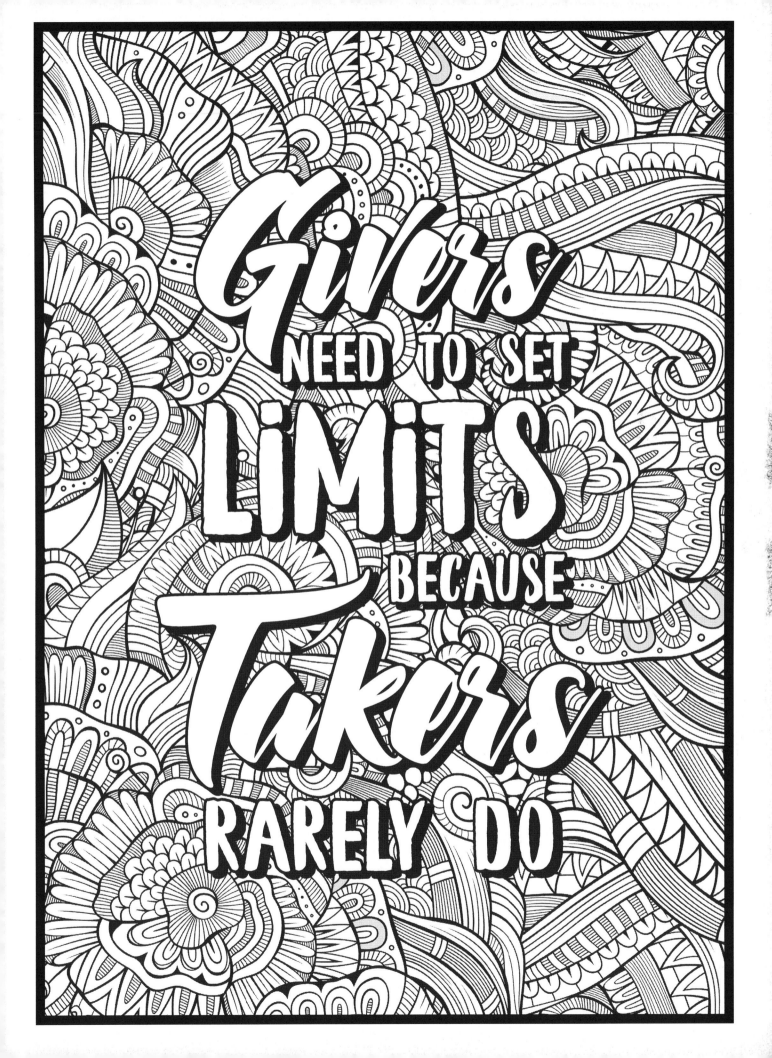

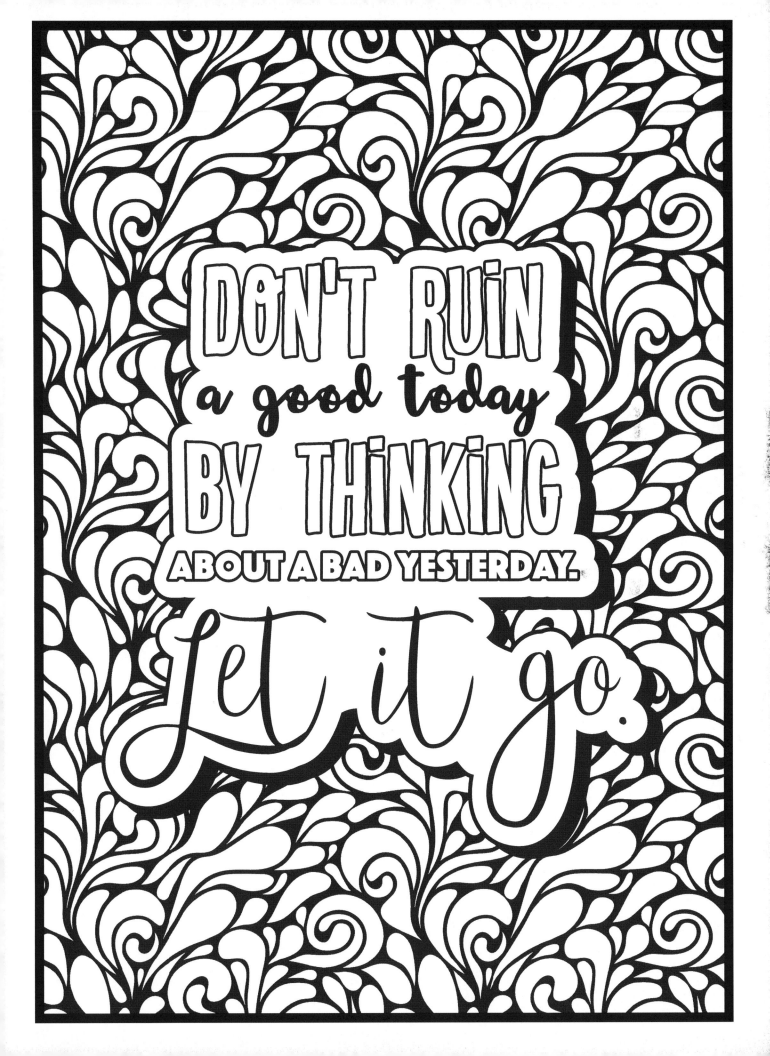

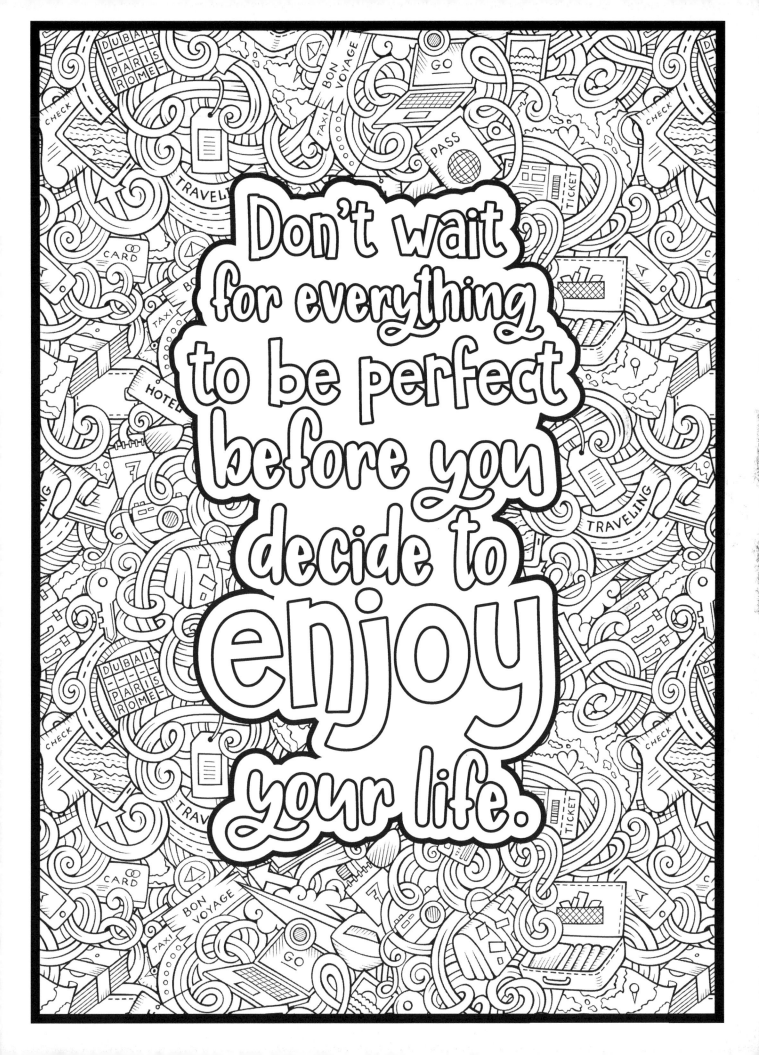

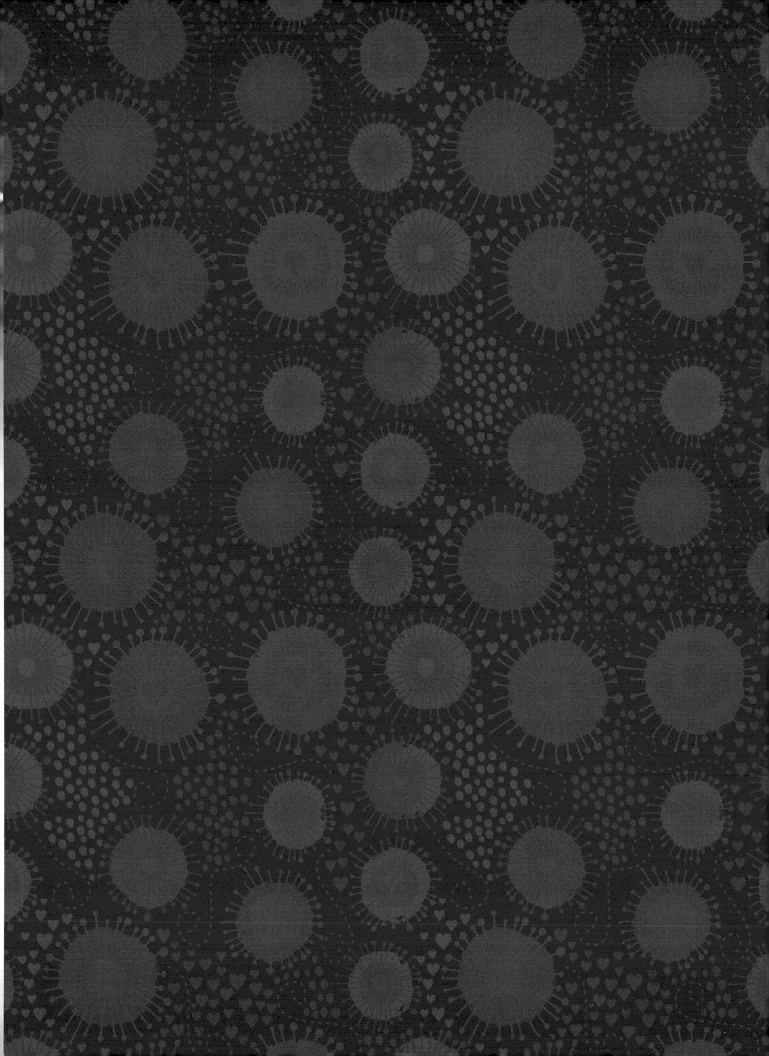

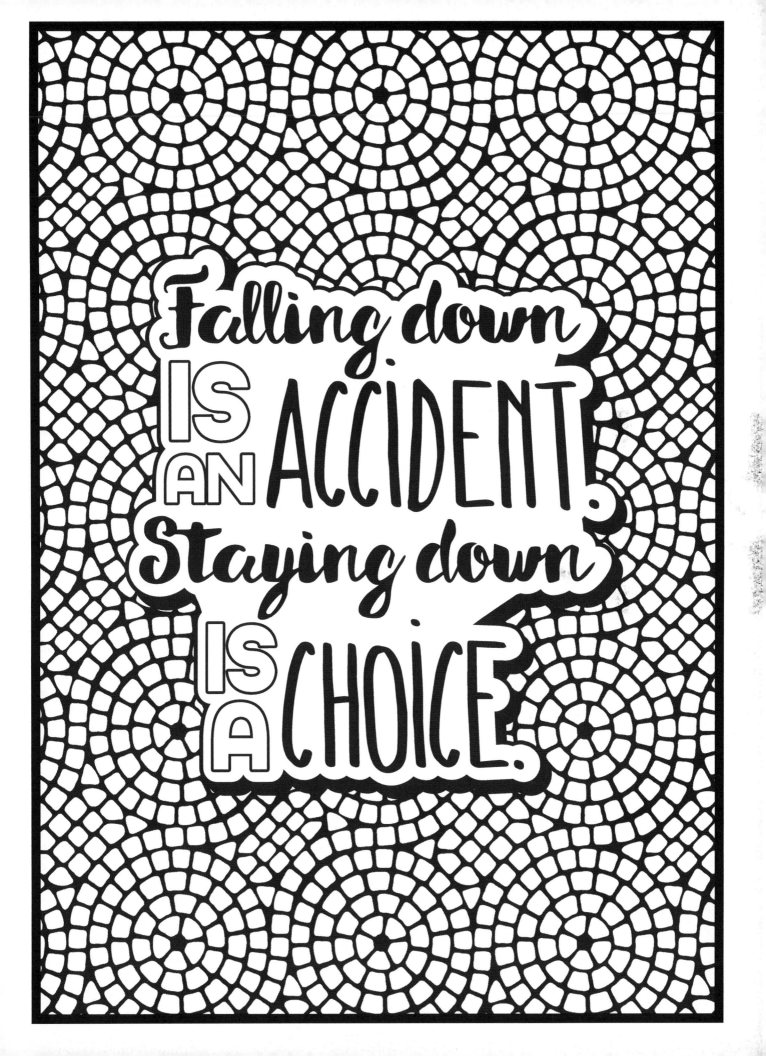

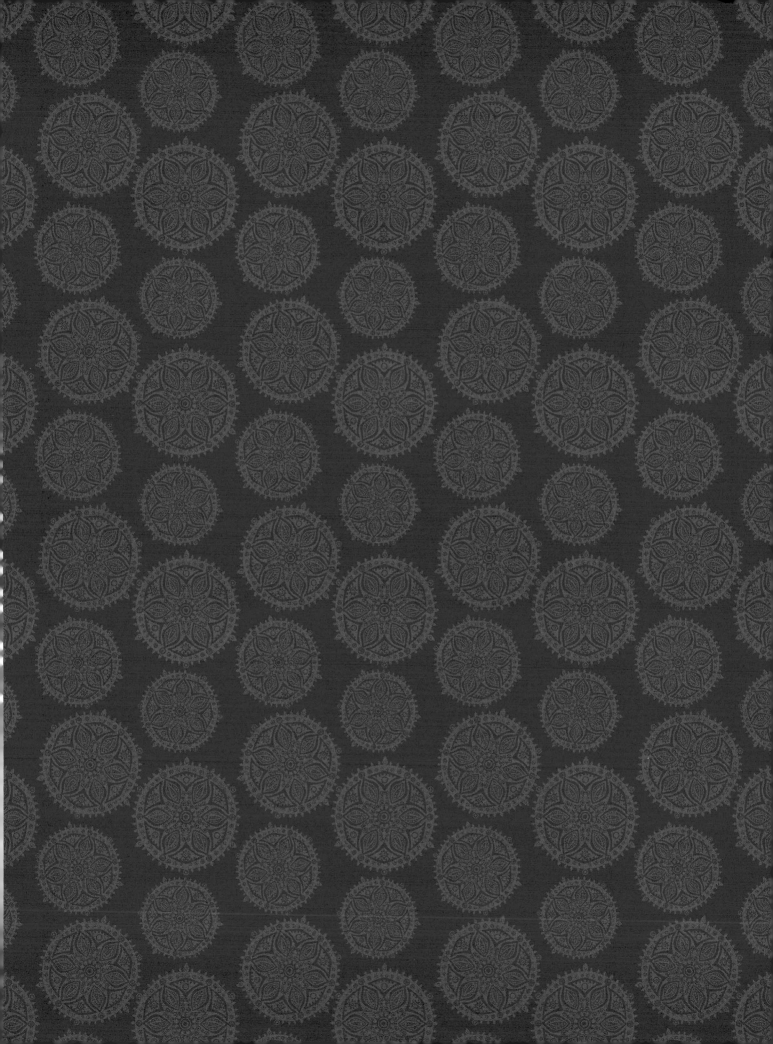

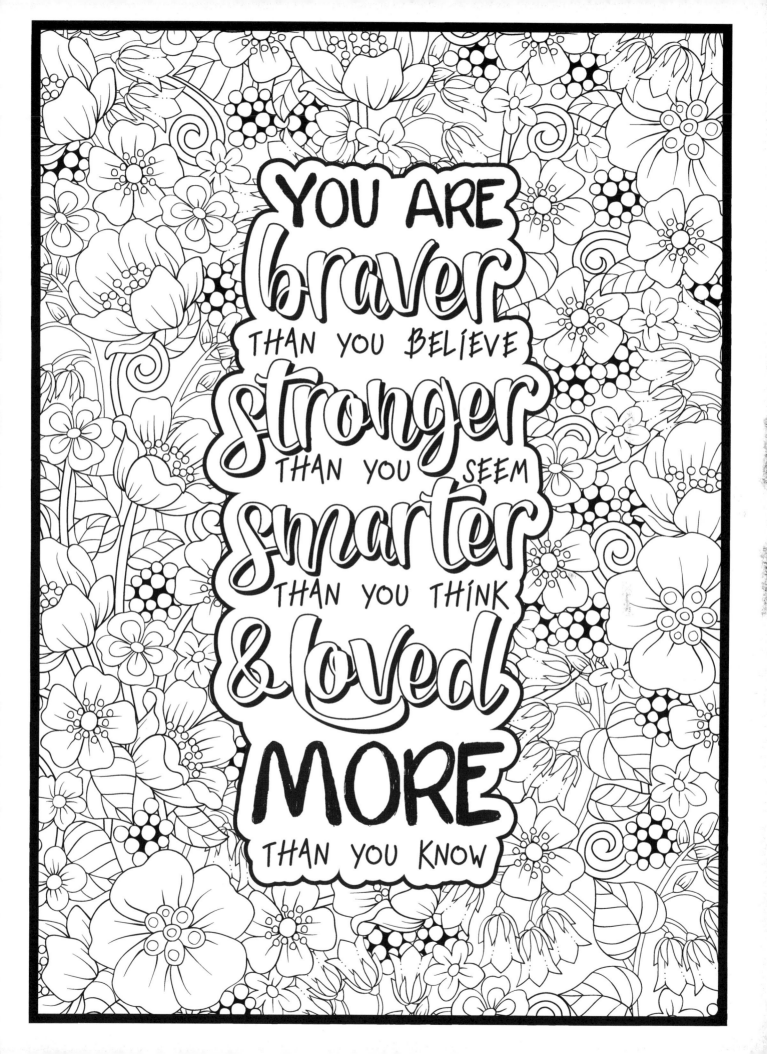

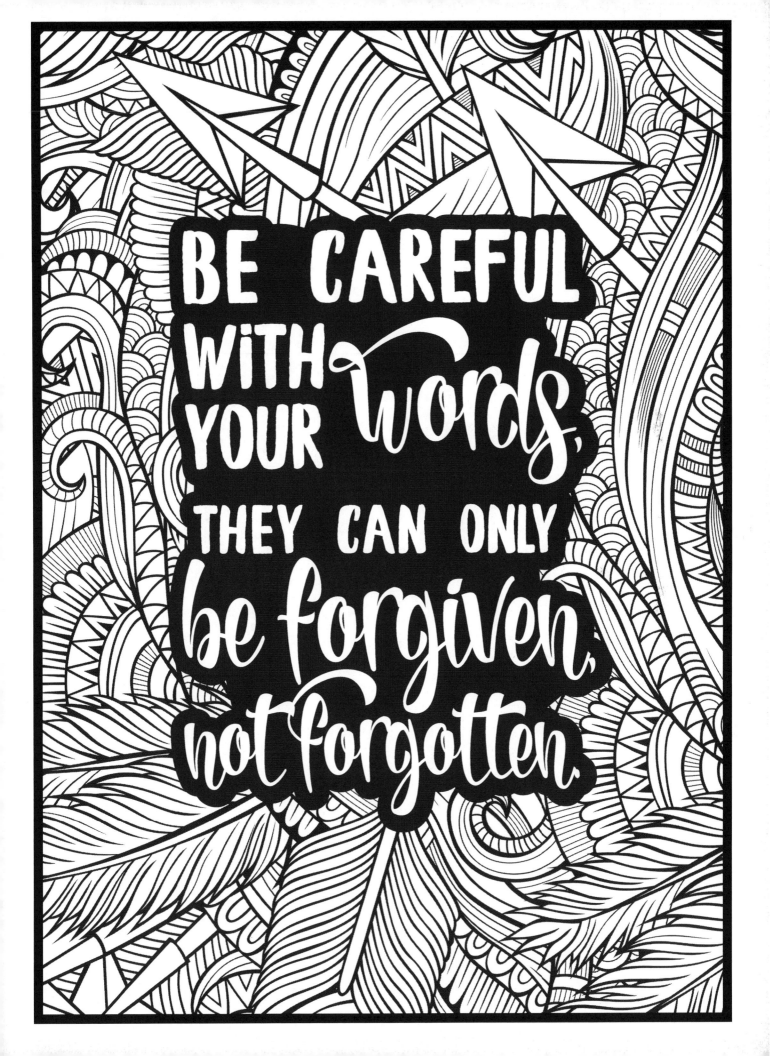

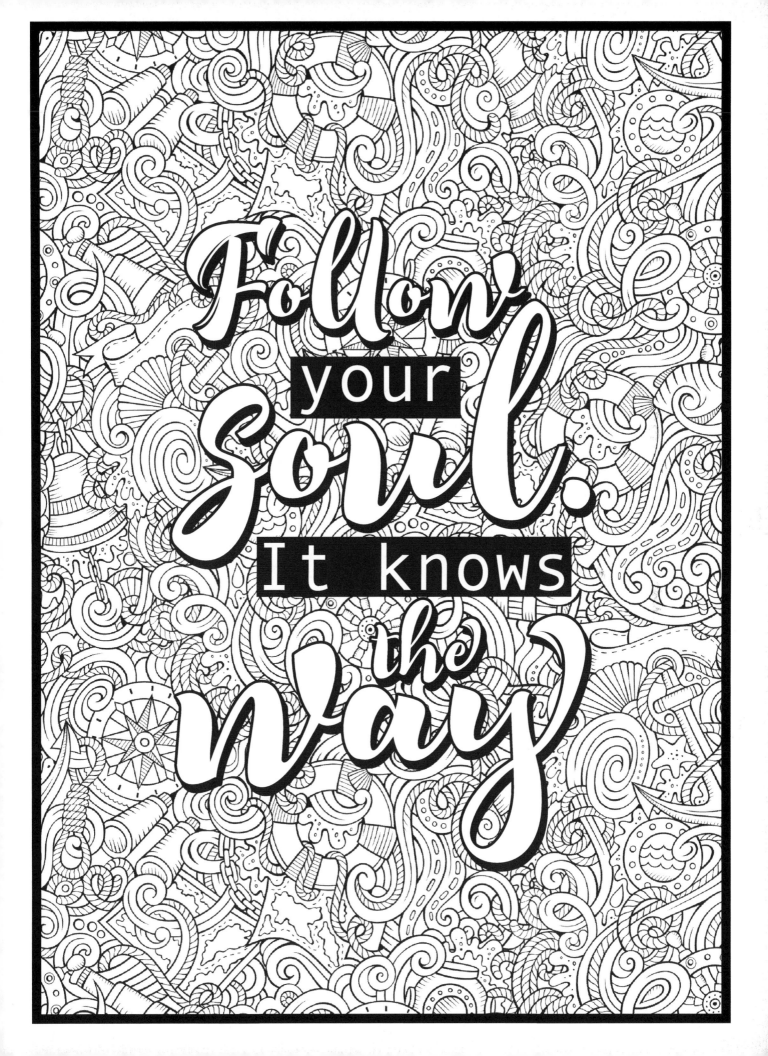

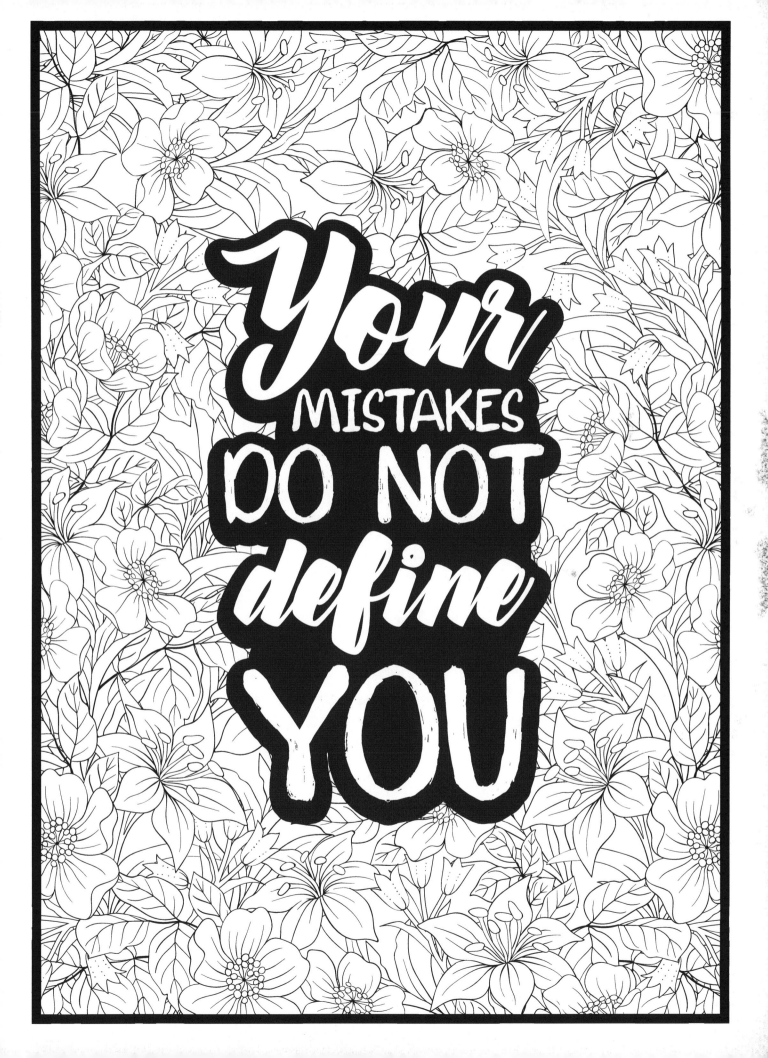

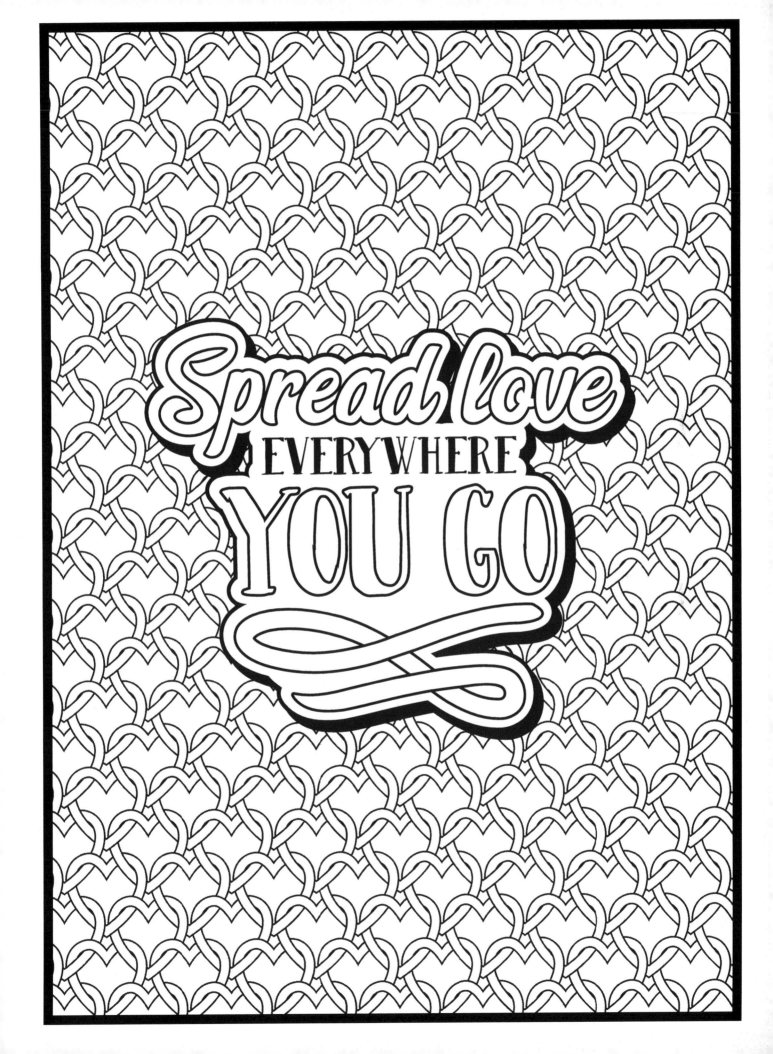

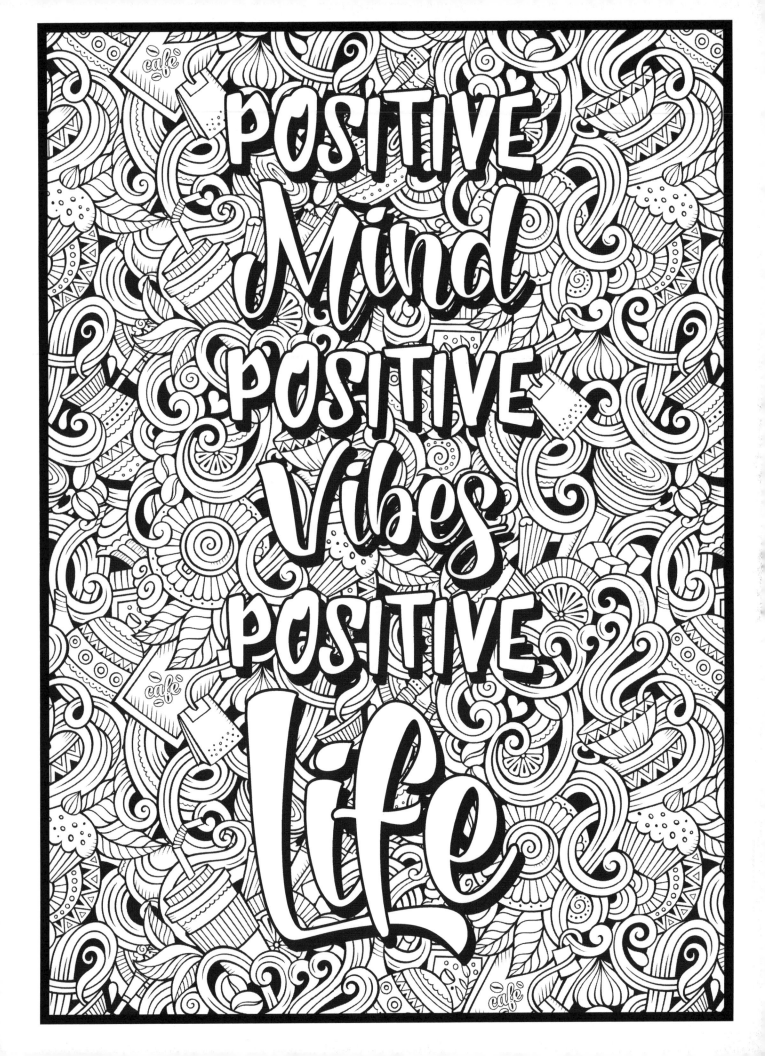

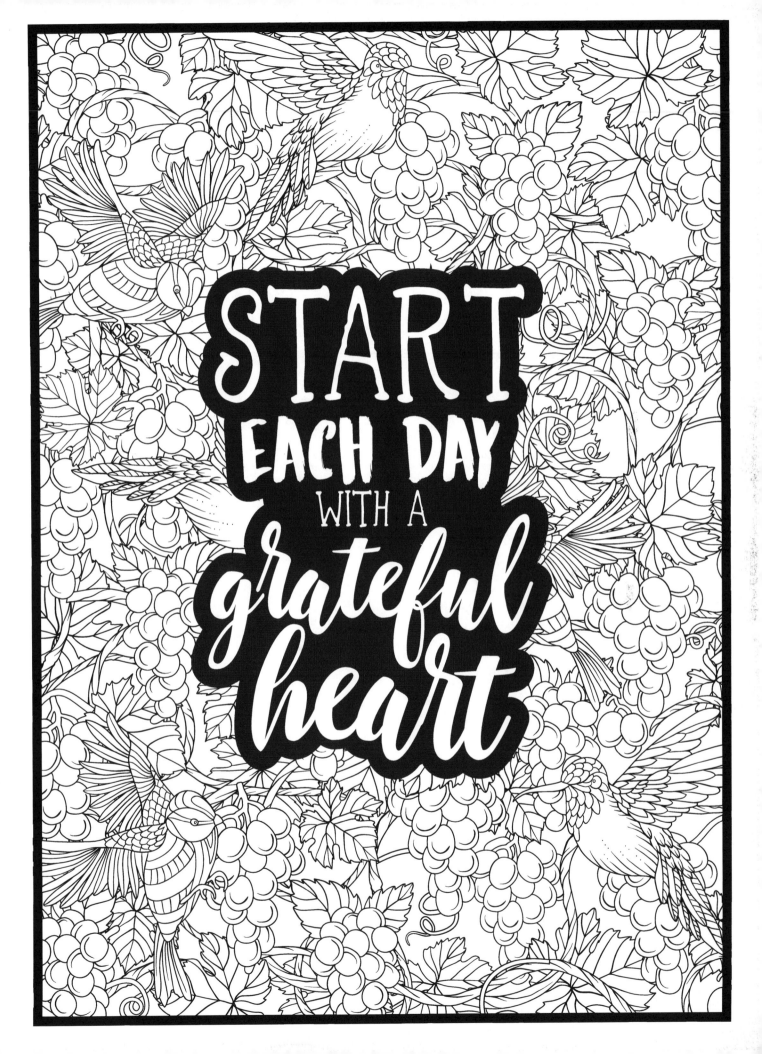

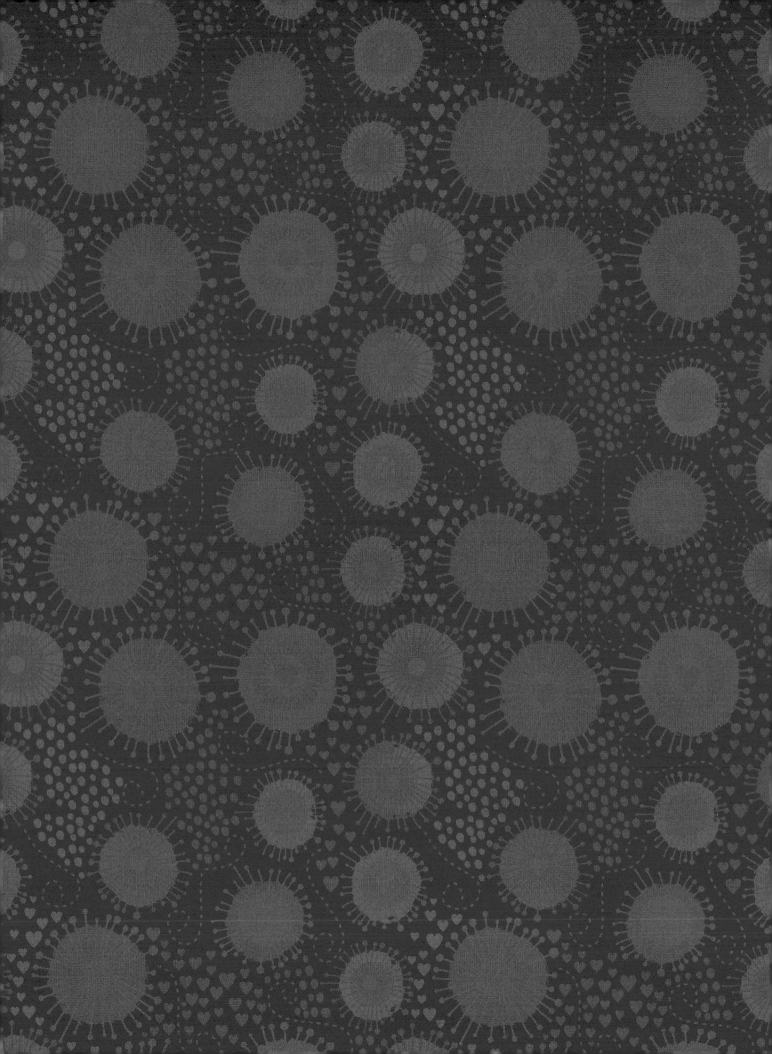

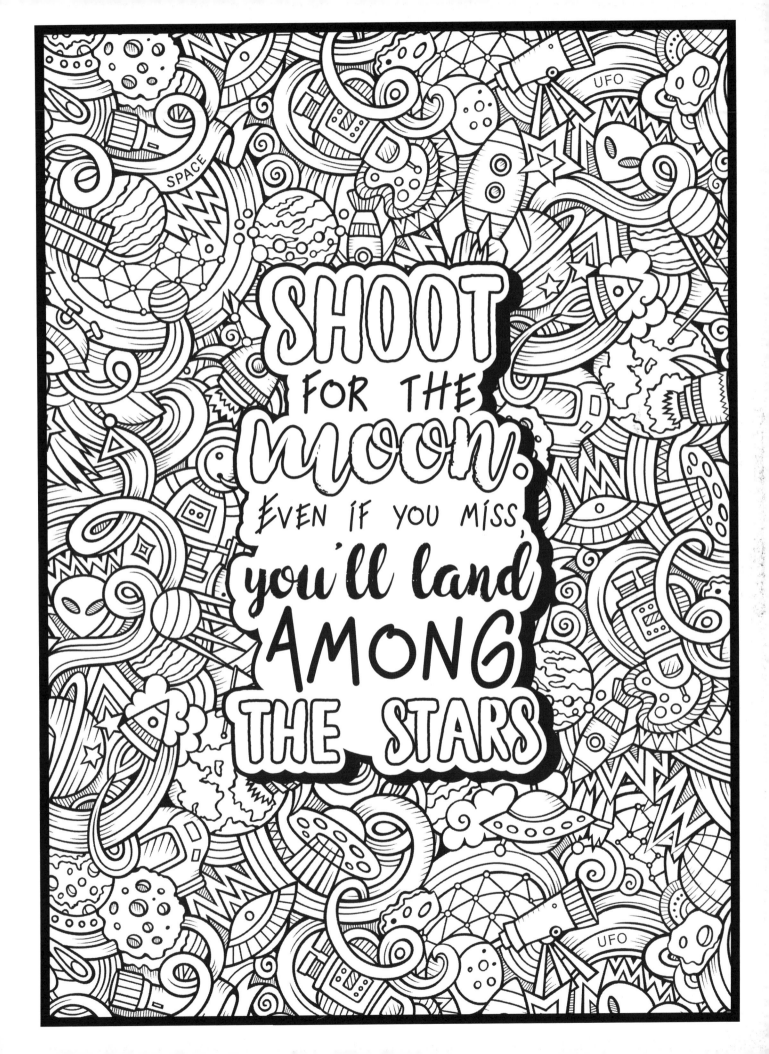

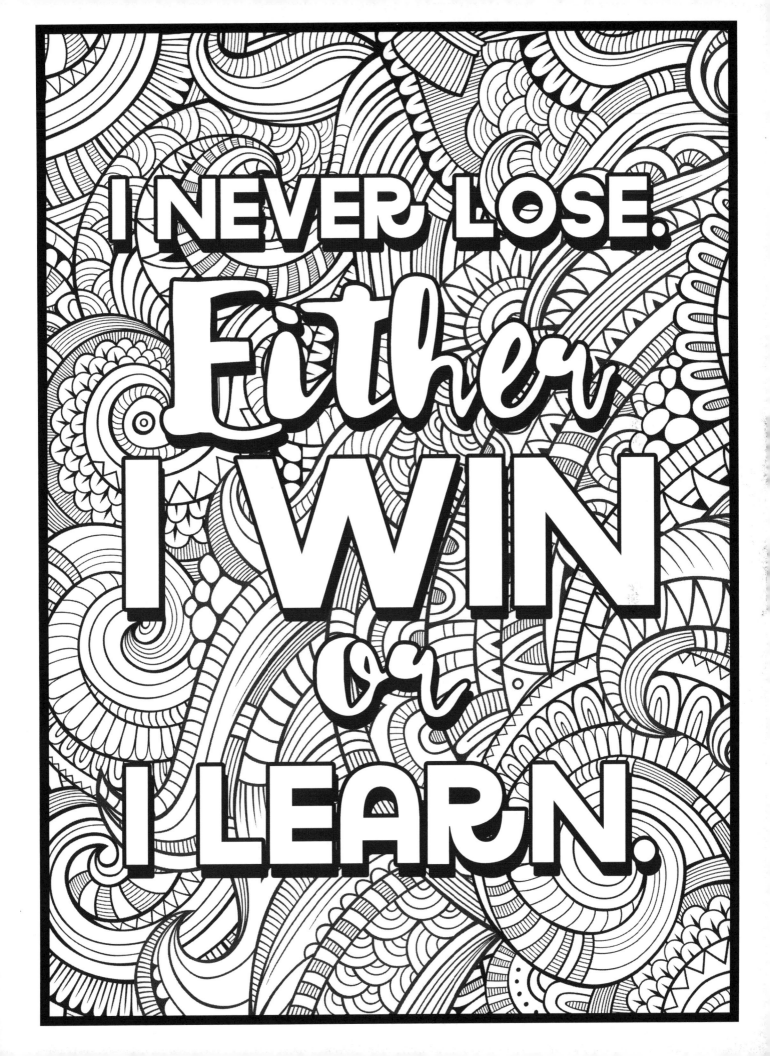

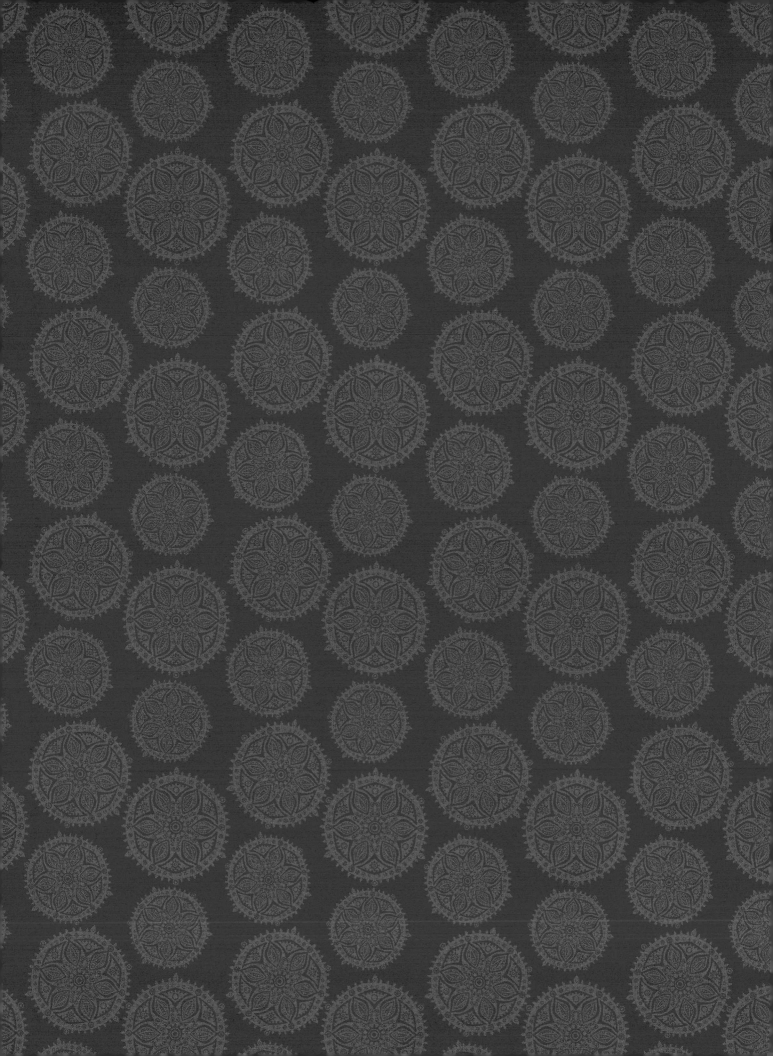

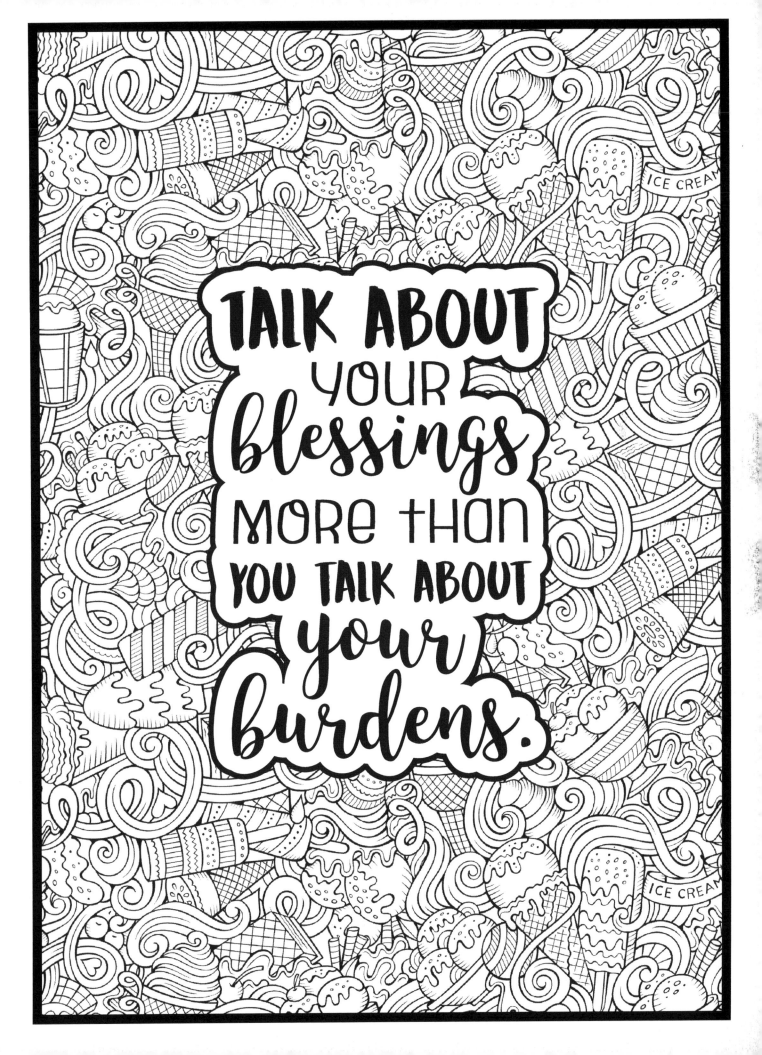

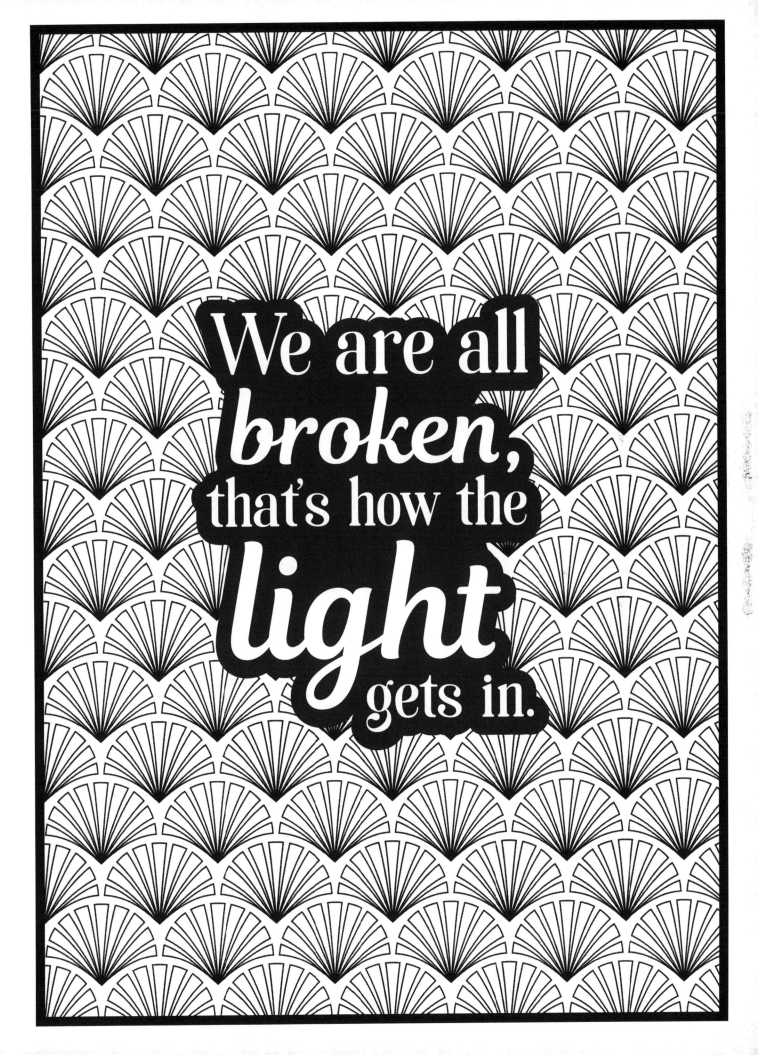

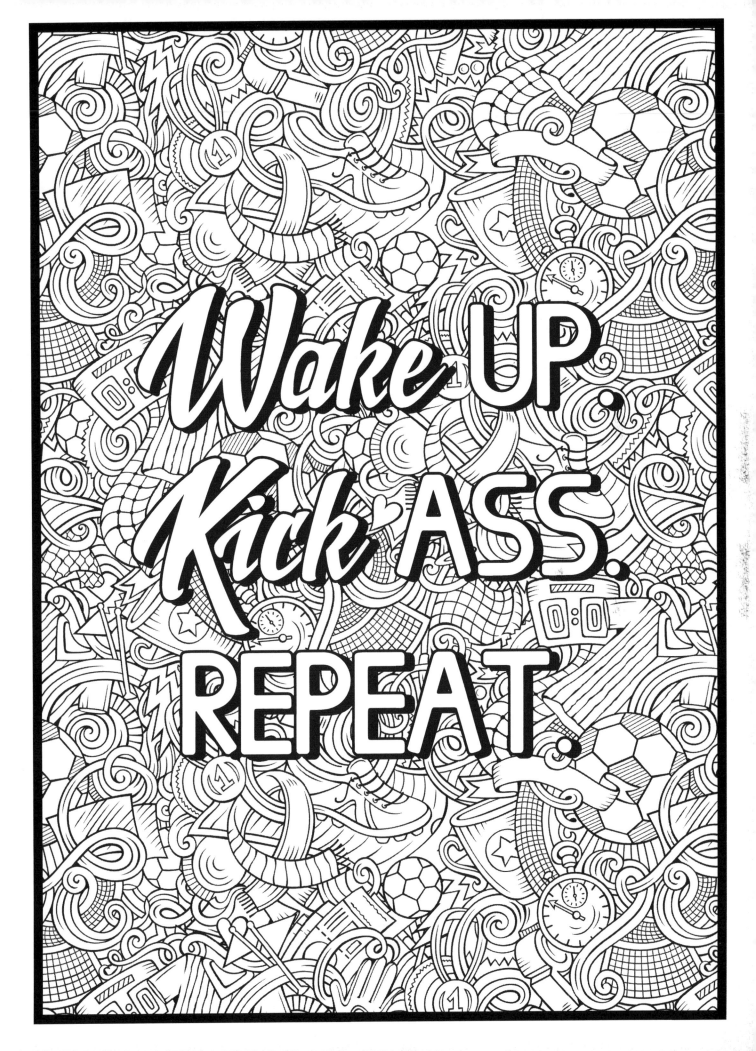

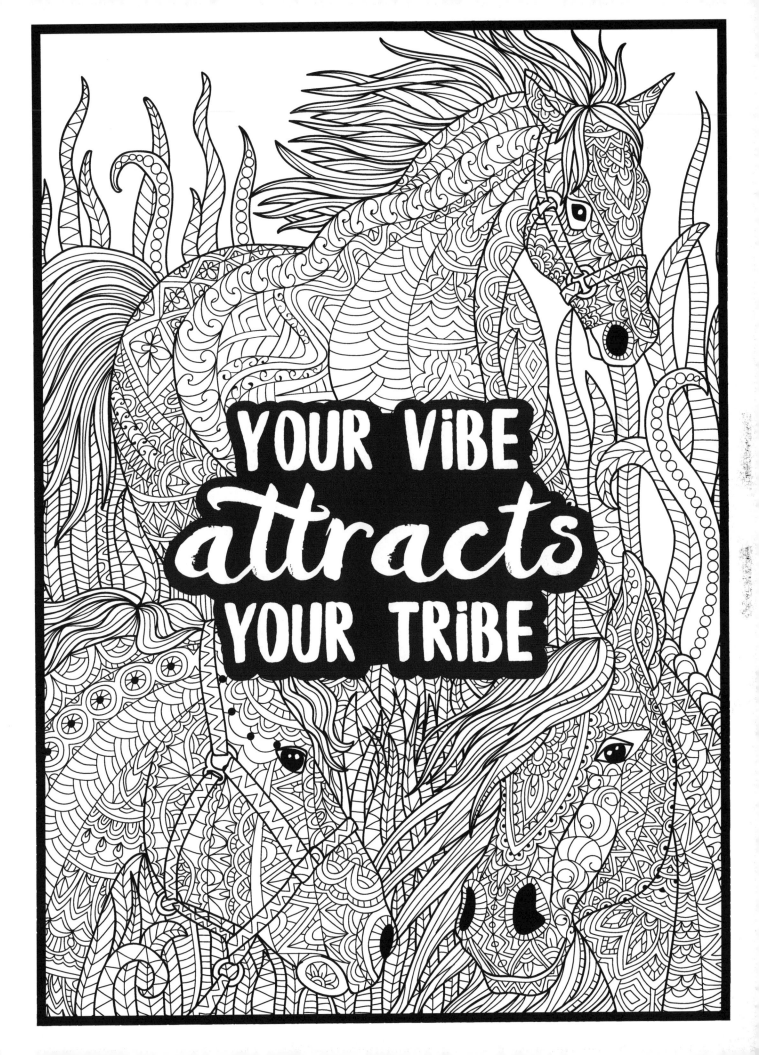

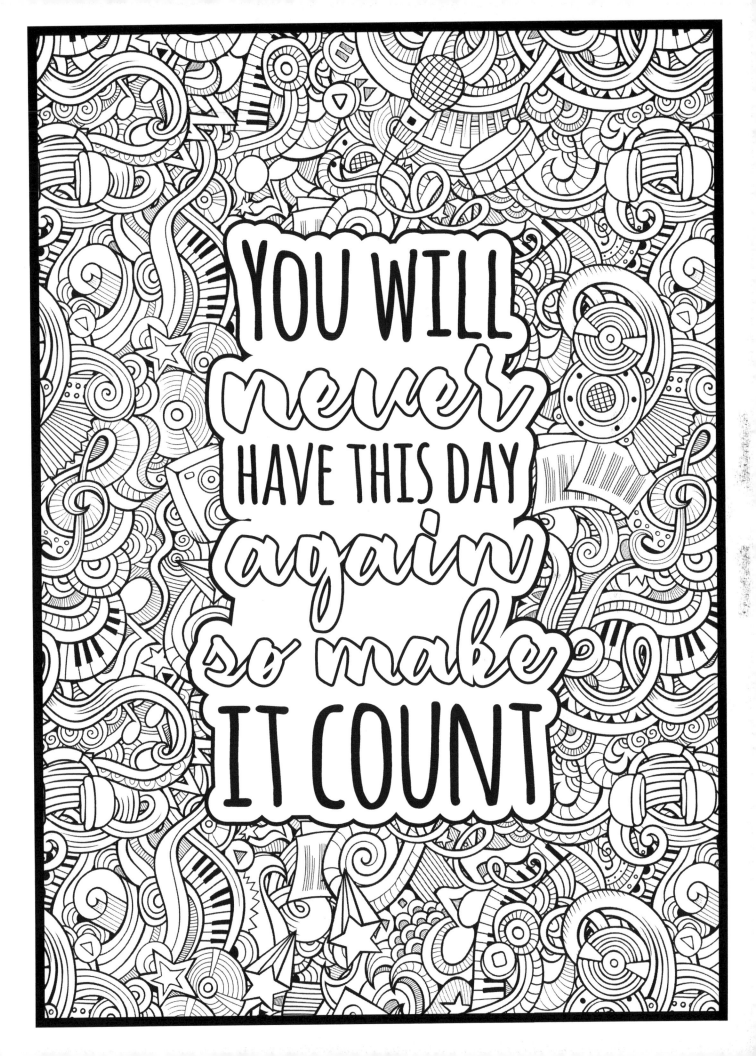

FREE PDF DOWNLOAD
OF THIS BOOK

Life is not about WAITING FOR the storm TO PASS BUT LEARNING to dance IN THE rain

Spread love EVERYWHERE YOU GO

Follow your soul. It knows the Way

www.pbleu.com/inspire

YOUR DOWNLOAD CODE: NP4569

@papeteriebleu

Papeterie Bleu

Want free goodies?
Email us at freebies@pbleu.com

@papeteriebleu

Papeterie Bleu

Shop our other books at
www.pbleu.com

Wholesale distribution through Ingram Content Group
www.ingramcontent.com/publishers/distribution/wholesale

For questions and customer service, email us at
support@pbleu.com

Made in the USA
Columbia, SC
08 April 2021